SOUL ROAD

By

I0151177

J. R. Canuel

A forward by Pastor Charles Allen

*Unless otherwise indicated, all Bible quotations
are taken from The King James Bible.*

ISBN# - 978-0-6151-3831-2
First printing January 2007
Published by Soul Road Publishing

Printed in the United States of America

SOUL ROAD

Introduction

The "soul" reason I created "Soul Road" was to guide others along their journey from the cradle to the grave. We all travel such different roads just to survive each day, but we all share the most important truth of all, the love of God. God wants each and every one of us to search for Him, reach out to Him, speak to Him, and then form a deep, personal and meaningful relationship with Him. The purpose of this book, is to help lead you down your own "Soul Road" and to strengthen your everlasting bond with "our" God.

It is my heartfelt prayer that you find one quiet moment at some point during your otherwise busy day, to allow God to enter your heart and to speak directly to you. I pray that at your leisure you will open this book to any particular page, and at that moment you will find direction and eternal inspiration.

I pray that "Soul Road" inspires you to "let the Holy Spirit do what the Holy Spirit do", or that in your life you "let God be God!"

Dedication

I dedicate "Soul Road", first and foremost to its true author, God! The words I write are not my own. I am merely a messenger relaying to you thoughts and inspiration from our Father.

To each and every member of my family, past and present, I could have never completed this book without your love, encouragement and patience.

A special thanks to Lacey. Thanks my baby girl for always being right by my side and bringing so much joy into my life.

Romans 1:9

For God is my witness, whom I serve with my spirit in the Gospel of His Son, that without ceasing I make mention of You always in my prayers.

"Let the Holy Spirit do,
What the Holy Spirit do!"
- J. R. Canuel-

Forward
By Pastor Charles Allen

"Soul Road" establishes the timeless theme of one's soul traveling through life in its endless search for truth and fulfillment. "Soul Road" invites you to open it to any page, anytime, anywhere, with the hope of softening your heart and allowing God to speak and direct you.

From the first lyric "What If?" to the very last poem "What I Believe", Joseph Canuel walks you through a sometimes exhaustive and frustrating search. Throughout our lives, with all its twists and turns, we seek important answers to the toughest questions in the "same old places." Rest assured that this book "Soul Road" is not one of those "same old places!" It is an exciting new way to discover where you stand in your relationship with God, and the wonders that lie ahead.

During our lives we walk through a curious maze of unanswered questions that challenge our very being. "How can my heart ever survive?" "Will my life make any difference?" "Will I ever find true happiness?" "Soul Road" will lead you to the answers to these questions, and beyond...

Joseph Canuel has with God's permission peered into the very soul of man in such a creatively lyrical and poetic way. He has presented us with an accurate picture of the soul of man and its life long quest to discover the truth and reality of God.

I pray that you read this with an open heart and mind, and that your "Soul Road" leads you to Jesus Christ and the hope of a new life in Him.

~Charles Allen~

Contents
Will There Ever Come a Day? Love Heals All

By Faith Alone

I'll Praise The Lord

1

Will There Ever Come a Day?

Will There Ever Come a Day?

Lord will my prayers,
Ever be heard on high?
And Lord will my tears,
Ever be wiped dry?

Lord will there ever come
Will there ever come a day?
When I will find the right prayers to pray?
Lord will there ever come,
Will there ever come a day?

Lord will my faith,
Ever be strong enough?
And Lord will my praise,
Ever lift You up?

Lord will there ever come,
Will there ever come a day?
When I will find the right prayers to pray?
Lord will there ever come,
Will there ever come a day?

Lord will my life,
Ever be lived for You?
And' Lord will my lies,
Ever know Your truth?

Lord will there ever come,
Will there ever come a day?
When I will find the right prayers to pray?
Lord will there ever come,
Will there ever come a day?

~ Canuel ~

1

Hard

Do we stand here so far apart?
Is there a true distance, now of the heart?
So just where do we start?

Has my doubt, held me here too long?
Has my weakness, again proved too strong?
Is there anywhere I now belong?

Lord I've already taken
Far too much of Your time
I've borrowed so many moments
That were never destined to be mine
I have asked You for Your favors
That I would return in kind
To one day have many secrets revealed
That have so far proved far too hard
Hard for me to find

So it seems the more I figure out
It seems the more, I now begin to doubt
Is there a clue, to what my life's about

Lord I do something, each and every day
That gives You every reason, to turn away
Its clear there's something here, much more at play

Lord I've already taken
Far too much of Your time
I've borrowed so many moments
That were never destined to be mine
I have asked You for Your favors
That I would return in kind
To one day have many secrets revealed
That have so far proved far too hard
Hard for me to find

I've tried to show You, just who I am
Then to convince You, just where I stand
That I'm far more, than this foolish man

I've laid before You, I have bared my soul
In search of answers, that only You could know
I am past the point I was afraid to go

I have tried to wish away my every sin
To bargain with You, over and over again
Why don't I feel any worse, here deep within?

~ Canuel ~

From Way Down Here

From way down here
Lord do You hear me pray?
Do You listen to a single word I say?
From way down here

From way down here
Lord do You feel my pain?
Do You know that my heart is okay?
From way down here

From way down here
Lord do You watch me fall?
Do You even notice me here at all?
From way down here

From way down here
Lord do You cry when I cry?
Do You hear my questions why?
From way down here

From way down here
I'm looking up for You Lord
With my eyes raised high
Looking up to the sky

From way down here
I'm reaching up for You Lord
With my arms raised high
Reaching up to the sky
From way down here

From way down here
Lord do You know how often I fail?
Do You warn me but to no avail?
From way down here

Do You want to get to know me?
Have You something to show me?
From way down here

Do You want to get my attention?
Is there something You're trying to tell me?
From way down here

From way down here
Lord do You speak to my heart?
Do You set my soul apart?
From way down here

~ Canuel ~

Watching Over You

Is there someone watching over me?
Got their hand upon my shoulder
Is there someone looking out for me?
As I grow now ever older

Is there someone there?
Is there someone here?
Watching over me?

My child, I'm watching over you
In your times of love, in the times to come
I'm watching over you
In your days of tears, in the times of fun
I'm watching over you

I'm watching you walk, watching you run
I'm watching you learn, then have just a little fun
I'm watching you rise, watching you fall
I'm watching you win, then maybe just lose it all

I'm watching you laugh, watching you cry
I'm watching you fail, then give just it another try
I'm watching you sing, watching you dance
I'm watching you hurt, then take just another chance

Is there someone watching over me?
Got their hand upon my shoulder
Is there someone guiding me?
As I grow now ever older

Is there someone there?
Is there someone here?
Watching over me?

My child, I'm watching over you
In your times of hurt, in the times that pass
I'm watching over you
In your days of tears, in the times that you'll laugh
I'm watching over you
My child, I'm watching over you

~ Canuel ~
4

There's a Still Small Voice

In the quiet of a moment
In the silence of a prayer
There's a still small voice
And it's whispering

In the new light of day
In the first breath of the wind
There's a still small voice
And it's whispering

In all of the thoughts in between
In the falling of just one tear
In all of the hurt unseen
In all of the days that now disappear

In the faith of a child
In the stillness of the night
There's a still small voice
And it's whispering

There's a still small voice

~ Canuel ~
5

Turn

Why do you turn?
Why do you turn away?
What's broken your heart?
What's broken your heart this day?

Do you ever look behind?
Do you ever look around?
Do you ever wonder?
If the loneliness ever makes a sound?

When even now
I would hold you close
For here between us
Would lie not a shadow

What makes you so sad?
What makes you so sad that you cry?
What's turned smile to tear?
What's turned smile to tears in blue eyes?

Do you ever want to run?
Do you ever need to hide?
Do you ever wonder?
If the truth is lurking close from behind?

When even now
I would hold you close
For here between us
Would lie not a shadow

Why do you turn?
Why do you turn away?

~ Canuel ~
6

The Dark and The Light

Father You taught the rains to dance
Placed the forests to stand tall

Father You willed the winds to sing
An' gave thunder, roar above them all

And the dark, to be night
And the day, to be light

Father You fashioned the oceans deep
Loosed the lightning across the sky

Father You formed the mountains strong
An' poised the eagle, ready to take flight

And the dark, to be night
And the day, to be light

An' like the wind
That now moves upon the water
Lord You breathe
Your life into this life

An' like the dew
That now rests upon the flower
Lord You breathe
Your life into this life

And the dark, to be night
And the day, to be light

~ Canuel ~

7

Feel

Do you really want to know, how I really feel?
I mean how I really, really feel
Do you really want to know, what lies deep inside?
I mean what lies really, deep inside

I want to show you, I want to know you
I want you to feel, the way I feel
I want to share you, I want to dare you
I want you to feel, the way I feel

Do you really want to know, what runs through my mind?
I mean what really runs wild, here through my mind
Do you really want to be a part of all I am?
I mean be a part of, all I am

I want to show you, I want to know you
I want you to feel, the way I feel
I want to share you, I want to dare you
I want you to feel, the way I feel

So tell me the truth, now are you listening?
Just don't tell me what I want to hear
This room's too quiet, now to be whispering
Don't be miles away, when I'm right here

Do you really want to look deep, within my soul?
I mean really look deep, here within my soul
Do you really want to warm, your heart next to mine?
I mean really warm your heart, here next to mine

I want to show you, I want to know you
I want you to feel, the way I feel
I want to share you, I want to dare you
I want you to feel, the way I feel

Do you really want to know what lies deep inside?
I mean what lies really, here deep inside

~ Canuel ~
8

Torn

Lord I am thankful, for today
And I pray, for tomorrow

But Lord I am tearful, for today
And I pray, for my sorrow

But I have torn away
Each and every layer
That I can tear away
I have prayed away
Each and every prayer
That I can kneel away

Lord I am mindful, for today
And I pray, for tomorrow

But Lord I am hopeful, for today
And I pray, for prayers I borrow

But I have torn away
Each and every layer
That I can tear away
I have prayed away
Each and every prayer
That I can kneel away

I will lay, I will lay aside
My every act of my human pride
That I've hidden well, I've kept here deep inside
And I will lay, I will lay apart
My every scar, from this wounded heart
Again hidden well, I've kept here far apart

Lord I am grateful, for today
And I pray, for tomorrow

But Lord I am careful, for today
And I pray, for whom I follow

But I have torn away
Each and every layer
That I can tear away
I have prayed away
Each and every prayer
That I can kneel away

Lord I am thankful, for today
And I pray, for tomorrow

~ Canuel ~
9

Here You Are Again

You've tried to keep inside
Every one of your tears
Tried so hard to hide
Every one of your fears

You've tried to break free
With nothing holding you down
Tried so hard to believe
With nothing but your doubt

And here you are again
Between your faith and your sin
Here you are again, here you are again

You've tried to run away
You didn't get too far
Tried so hard pray
You didn't how to start

You've tried to hold on
It was best just to let go
Tried so hard to be strong
It was best just not to know

And here you are again
Between your faith and your sin
Here you are again, here you are again

You've tried to
Tried so hard to

And here you are again
Between your faith and your sin
Here you are again, here you are again

~Canuel~
10

I Will Give You My Hand

You may now be falling
You may already be down
You may now be trying
To get back up off the ground

You may now be leaving
You may already be gone
You may now be hurting
Just so tired of being alone

**My child I will lift you up
I will help you stand
I will not let you fall
I will give you my hand
I will give you my hand**

You may now be searching
You may already feel lost
You may now be thinking
How can I ever now pay this cost?

So you may now be crying
So you may already feel sad
So you may now be blaming
Each and every love you've ever had

*Lord I'm kneeling here tonight
Lord I'm feeling, far from all right
Lord I'm in need of a little prayer tonight
But Lord I'm healing, here in Your light
Lord I'm healing, here in Your light*

**My child I will lift you up
I will help you stand
I will not let you fall
I will give you my hand**

I will give you my hand

~ *Canuel* ~

11

What If?

What if I'm not ready?
What if I'm not there?

What if I am found too late?
That's what this soul fears

What if I'm lost?
I'm lost and never found

What if You come and go?
Just as You said without a sound

From my knees, to this heart
From my soul, from the start
I don't want to be left apart

What if I've had the choice?
And I have chosen wrong

What if I've had the time?
And I have taken too long

What if I've been shown the road?
Yet I made my own way

What if I've been whispered words?
And still had my own say

From my knees, to this heart
From my soul, from the start
I don't want to be left apart

I'm covered by my own worthless reasons
Smothered by my own selfish treasons
Imprisoned by my own chains of flesh and bone
Barricaded by my own walls of stone

What if I drift further away?
And never find my way home
What if I cannot break free?
And end this journey alone

~ Canuel ~
12

A Better Man

Everyday I get on my knees and I pray
Every night I ask You, to be my guide
Everyday I do my best just to make my way
Every night I thank You, as I turn off the light

Lord please, give me Your hand
Help my heart, understand
Lord I want to be, a better man

Everyday I search Your words, for the words to say
Every night I ask You, to choose what's right
Everyday I try hard, not to fall away
Every night I pray to You, for another reason to try

Lord please, give me Your hand
Help my heart, understand
Lord I want to be, a better man

Lord Your hope brings, to me hope
And Your faith brings, to me faith
Lord Your love brings, to me love
And Your strength brings, to me strength
Lord it brings to me strength

Lord please, give me Your hand
Help my heart, understand
Lord I want to be, a better man

Everyday I get on my knees and I pray
Every night I thank You, as I turn off the light

~ Canuel ~

It's Christmas Out There

Maybe it's the new fallen snow lying on the ground
Or maybe it's the gifts placed under the tree that I've found
Or maybe it's the bells ringing in the little church downtown
Maybe it's that time of year, maybe its Christmas out there

Maybe it's just Santa there waving at the old Wilson's store
Or maybe it's the brand new wreath
Hanging now on my front door
Or maybe it's that everyone now seems to care just a little more
Maybe it's that time of year, maybe its Christmas out there

An' there's just no other feeling
Than when the spirit comes alive
There's just no, better feeling
Than when you feel His love inside
Maybe it's that time of year
Maybe it's Christmas out there

Maybe it's the manger scene placed under Main Streets lights
Or maybe it's the choir now singing all their praise tonight
Or maybe it's the Salvation Army Band playing "Silent Night"
Maybe it's that time of year, maybe its Christmas out there

An' there's just no other feeling
Than when the spirit comes alive
There's just no, better feeling
Than when you feel His love inside
Maybe it's that time of year
Maybe it's Christmas out there

Yes it's Christmas out there

~ Canuel ~
14

Bring Me Closer Today

How do You know my name?
How do You hear me cry, when I'm alone?

How do You feel my hurt?
How do You know my heart, when nothings shown?

When I'm so far away
Much farther than just yesterday
To bring me nearer, is what I pray
To bring me closer
Bring me closer today

How do You talk to me?
How do You speak so I'll understand?

How do You hear me here?
How do You always know just where I am?

Although I tried to hide
And keep all my fears deep inside
You reached to me, wiped all my tears, just as I cried

Although I tried to run
From all I've either said or done
You knelt beside me
Prayed then with me
Together just as one

So when I'm so far away
Much further than just yesterday
To bring me nearer is what I pray
To bring me closer today

Lord bring me closer today

~ *Canuel* ~
15

No Matter How Far

No matter how far I fall
Your arms are there to hold me
To raise me to where You are

No matter how far I crawl
Your love is there to find me
To bring me to where You are
To bring me home, to make me Your own
No matter how far

Oh Lord, how I've fallen
It seems so many times
Lord I've been crawling
Right here before Your very eyes

More than anything
I want to listen and hear Your words
More than anything
I want to be still and to learn

More than anything
I want to be in prayer, and on my knees
More than anything
I want to know Your love, and to believe

No matter how far I fall
Your arms are there to hold me
To raise me to where You are
No matter how far I fall

No matter how far

~ *Canuel* ~
16

In The Silence of A Prayer

I must say, a thousand times a day
Why, God, why?
Why must my heart still cry?

I must pray, a thousand times a day
When, God, when?
When will I ever smile again?

And then here, in the silence of a prayer
In the quiet of a moment
You speak to me

Then here, in the stillness of the night
In the calm before dawn
You whisper to me
In the silence of a prayer

I must say, a thousand times a day
How, God, how?
How will I ever make it now?

I must pray, a thousand times a day
Where, God, where?
Where does my soul go from here?

Only when I am still
And I am all alone
You make Yourself known

Only when I am still
When I am down upon my knees
You put my lost soul at ease
In the silence of a prayer

I must say, a thousand times a day
Who, God, Who?
Who can I now reach for You?

And then here, in the silence of a prayer
In the quiet of a moment
You speak to me

Then here, in the stillness of the night
In the calm before dawn
You whisper to me
In the silence of a prayer

~ Canuel ~
17

If You Pray

So today there is rain
Tomorrow the skies will clear again

So today there is hurt
Tomorrow your heart will feel joy again

Tomorrow there'll be no more rain
Tomorrow there'll be no more hurt

If you pray
Faith will win the day

If you pray
Love will find a way
Into your heart, into your soul
Into your life
If you pray

So today there are storms
Tomorrow the seas will calm again

So today there is doubt
Tomorrow your hope will rise again

Tomorrow there'll be no more storms
Tomorrow there'll be no more doubt

If you pray
Faith will win the day

If you pray
Love will find a way
Into your heart, into your soul
Into your life
If you pray

Kneeling down, all alone
Giving all, all you own
If you pray

~ Canuel ~
18

You Won't Need Your Wallet

We all go to school, just to learn what?
How best to make more money, to move on up
But when you knock upon the door
"I'm coming!" says the Lord
You won't need your wallet anymore

So you put in more hours, just to gain what?
A BMW, is that's what you want?
But when you look in the window
"Come around front!" says the Lord
You won't need your wallet anymore

You won't need your wallet anymore
The Lord don't take no cash or credit that's for sure
You'll have to check your faith right there at the door
You won't need your wallet anymore

You climb up the ladder, just to get where?
Rung by rung, right up until there's nothing there
So when you ring that bell, "Come on inside!" says the Lord
You won't need your wallet anymore

You won't need your wallet anymore
The Lord don't take cash or credit that I'm sure
You'll have to check your faith right there at the door
You won't need your wallet anymore

I know this goes, against all we know
A little secret the world doesn't want to show
That you take nothing with you
When it s time for you to leave
Just who you are, and what you believe
What you believe!!

You won't need your wallet anymore
The Lord don't take cash or credit that I'm sure
You'll have to check your faith right there at the door
You won't need your wallet anymore

You won't need your wallet anymore

~ Canuel ~
19

Stronger

Stronger, my faith needs to be a little stronger
Longer, my faith needs to last a little longer

But Lord I give up, far too easy
Lord I give in, much too quickly
Lord fill me with Your grace
Fill me with Your strength
Lord make me stronger

Harder, my faith needs to work a little harder
Farther, my faith needs to reach a little farther

But Lord I give up, far too easy
Lord I give in, much too quickly
Lord fill me with Your grace
Fill me with Your strength
Lord make me stronger

Make me stronger today
Lord somehow, tomorrow's so far away
Stronger today
Lord right now, tomorrow's a brand new day
Lord make me stronger

Clearer, my faith needs to see a little clearer
Nearer, my faith needs to draw a little nearer

But Lord I give up, far too easy
Lord I give in, much too quickly
Lord fill me with Your grace
Fill me with Your strength
Lord make me stronger

~ Canuel ~

The Gift

My Lord You've offered me
Faith for this faithless soul

My Lord You have shown me
Hope for this hopeless world

Lord what have I to offer You?
But my recklessness, my fear
Lord what would You now have me do?
To keep You close, right here

My Lord You've given me
Grace for this graceless life

My Lord You've revealed to me
Truth for this truth less heart

Lord why do I still turn away?
Time and time again
Lord what would You now have me say?
To pray with You my friend,
To pray with You my friend

Lord what have I to offer You?
But my recklessness, my fear
Lord what would You now have me do?
To keep You close right here

My Lord You've offered me
Faith for this faithless soul

~ Canuel ~
21

It's Alright

It's alright, to raise your hands
To lift your praise to the Lord

It's alright, as you reach up high
To lift your dreams to the Lord

It's alright, it's alright

It's alright, if you feel afraid
To give your fears to the Lord

It's alright, now if you cry
To give your tears to the Lord

It's alright, it's alright

It's alright, when you look to the sky
To lift your soul to the Lord

It's alright, as you open your heart
To lift your life to the Lord

It's alright, it's alright

It's alright, as you kneel
To give your prayers to the Lord

It's alright, as you close your eyes
To give your cares to the Lord

It's alright, it's alright

~ Canuel ~
22

When There's Faith

Tears dry, hurts healed
When there's faith

Mountains move, truths revealed
When there's faith

When there's faith
You'll believe the unbelievable
When there's faith
You'll reach the unreachable
When there's faith

Doubts fade, hopes raised
When there's faith

Hearts sing, souls saved
When there's faith

When there's faith
Your soul will sing a new song
When there's faith
Your soul will find it's home
When there's faith

Tears dry, hurts healed
When there's faith

When there's faith
You'll believe the unbelievable
When there's faith
You'll reach the unreachable
When there's faith

~ Canuel ~
23

Never Again

How do I find my way?
Have the right words to say, find a quiet place to pray?

How am I to change my mind?
To now take the time, leave my every sin behind?

How am I to let go?
Of all that I know, all I ever was before?

How am I to hold onto?
All these things new, an' keep my eyes upon only You?

And never again, to turn away
From You my friend
And never again, to lose my way
From You my friend
No, never again

How do I see the light?
To always know what's right, an' hold You here in my sight?

How can I not go wrong?
Never take too long, an' find the strength to somehow be strong

Then I'm to step out in faith
Stand up in praise and my arms I raise

Then I'm to lift up my eyes
Cast my cares to the sky, never will we say goodbye
Never again!

No never again, am I to turn away
From You my friend
And never again, am I to lose my way
From You my friend
No, never again, never again

~ Canuel ~
24

Grace

But for Your Grace
This soul would be left to wander

But for Your Grace
By these chains of sin I'd be bound

But for Your Grace
I'd be just a shadow, this I wonder

But for Your Grace
I'd be lost, never found

**It is only by Your word
That I am moved
Nothing I do on my own
Can that prove**

**For it is only by Your Grace
That I am saved
Nothing I do, on my own
Can that change
Can that change**
Grace...

~ Canuel ~
25

2

Love Heals All

Love Heals All

Word after word, we speak
And truth after truth, still we seek

Tear after tear, we cry
And time after time, still we try

**Whenever right, it threatens wrong
Love heals all**

Pain after pain, we feel
And hurt after hurt, still we heal

Prayer after prayer, we pray
And time after time, still we stay

**Whenever weak, it battles strong
Love heals all**

*So with now just a prayer
With all that one heart can bear
With our eyes lifted high
With now every tear, to be wiped dry*
Love heals all

So heart after heart, we ache
And step after step, still we take

Hope after hope, we raise
And time after time, still we praise

**Whenever time, it takes too long
Love heals all**

~ Canuel ~
26

Need

Lord I need Your love
To see me through my blindness

Lord I need Your light
To lead me through my darkness

Lord I need Your love
Lord I need Your light

Lord I need Your grace
To take me through my helplessness

Lord I need Your hope
To bring me through my loneliness

Lord I need Your grace
Lord I need Your hope
Lord I need Your love
Lord I need Your light

Lord I need Your faith
To lift me through my brokenness

Lord I need Your love
Lord I need Your light

~ Canuel ~
27

I Will Lift My Eyes

In the hardest of times
I will lift my eyes to you Lord
In the moments I am tired
I will lift my eyes to you Lord

Through every tear that I cry
Through my every question why
I will lift my eyes

In the darkest of nights
I will lift my eyes to you Lord

In the moments I am tried
I will lift my eyes to you Lord

Through every prayer that I pray
To my every promise made
I will lift my eyes

I will lift my eyes to you Lord

Through every tear that I cry
Through my every question why
I will lift my eyes

Every moment I'm awake
And every breath that I take
I will lift my eyes

~ Canuel ~
28

My Hearts Desire

Lord I want to be with You
I want to now see You
Lord I want Your love

I want to stand here beside You
I want to now feel You
Lord I want Your love

With my hearts desire
To live all that You've laid out for me
And my hearts desire
To live all that You've promised, my life to be

Lord I want to walk with You
Be close now to You
Lord I want Your love

I want to sing out now to You
Pray here now with You
Lord I want Your love

Lord I want to reach, reach out to You
Be held gently in Your arms
I want to cry, cry out to You
Be kept safe and free from harm
Free from harm

With my hearts desire
To live all that You've laid out for me
And my hearts desire
To live all that You've promised, my life to be

Lord I want to be with You
Be close now to You
Lord I want Your love

~ Canuel ~
29

Most of All

Sometimes I have no idea what You're thinking
And other times I have such a hard time just believing
Yet I'm kneeling before You now praying hard
It just doesn't seem that I'm getting very far

Most times I feel like it's far I've fallen
And other times it seems no one hears me calling
Yet I'm kneeling before You now praying here
Am I so afraid to admit to You that I still fear?

Most of all, Lord I pray
That You're here with me now praying
Most of all, that You're here at my side, right by my side

Most of all, Lord I pray
That You hear me now saying
That I'm not just along for the ride, along for the ride

I want to do more, I want to be more
I want to love more, I want to cry just a little more

I want to feel more, I want to live more
Lord I want to pray more, I want to believe just a little more
Just a little more!

At times I feel that all alone here as I'm traveling
And other times I know, that it's me that You're now carrying

Most of all, Lord I pray
That You're here with me now praying
Most of all, that You're here at my side, right by my side

Most of all, Lord I pray
That You hear me now saying
That I'm not just along for the ride, along for the ride

Lord I pray for this, most of all

~ Canuel ~
30

Here

No more hurt, no more pain
No more loneliness, no more hate
There is only love
There is only love, here, here

No more guilt, no more shame
No more emptiness, no more blame
There is only grace
There is only grace, here, here

I will bring You gifts, Lord of my love
I will sing You sings, Lord of my hope
I will bring You prayers, Lord faith
I will sing You songs
Lord of my soul, here, here

No more lies, no more tears
No more darkness, no more fears
There is only faith
There is only faith, here, here

I will bring You gifts, Lord of my love
I will sing You sings, Lord of my hope
I will bring You prayers, Lord faith
I will sing You songs,
Lord of my soul, here, here

~ Canuel ~
31

Faith

We all need to pray, just a little more
To lift our eyes high, high towards heavens door!
To step out in this world in faith

We all need to hope, just a little more
To lift our hearts high, have our spirits soar!
To step out in this world in faith

And to be found in grace
And just as a child found in faith

We all need to cry, just a little more
To lift our eyes high, forget what was before!
To step out in this world in faith

We all need to sing, just a little more
To lift our song high, out loud what we feel for!
To step out in this world in faith

And to be found in grace
And just as a child found in faith

We all need to hurt, just a little more
To lift our pain high, high above the roar!
To step out in this world in faith

And to be found in grace
And just as a child found in faith

We all need to believe, just a little more
To lift our faith high, higher than ever before!
To step out in this world in faith

And to be found in grace
And just as a child found in faith

~ Canuel ~

To The Cross

When my soul is aching
When my heart is breaking
I lift my eyes to the cross

When my hopes are fading
When my strength is straining
I lift my eyes to the cross to the cross

An' when I am lonely
When I am on my own
When I am lonely
When I'm so very far from home
Yes when I am lonely
When I am so very much alone
I lift my eyes, yes I lift my eyes
To the cross, to the cross

When my tears are flowing
When my fears are showing
I lift my eyes to the cross
And when my faith is failing
When my doubt is gaining
I lift my eyes to the cross, to the cross

An' when I am lonely
When I am on my own
When I am lonely
When I'm so very far from home
Yes when I am lonely
When I am so very much alone
I lift my eyes, yes I lift my eyes
To the cross, to the cross

~Canuel~
33

If I Fall Away

My Lord enter me
Please now open my eyes to see

My Lord draw me near
Please now open my ears to hear

But if I fall away, never further than today
It is for Your grace I pray, if I fall away

My Lord stand close by
Please remain, never leave my side

My Lord seek my heart
Please find me faithful, set me apart

But if I fall away, never further than today
It is for Your grace I pray, if I fall away
If I fall away

My Lord whisper truth
Please now touch, have my faith renewed

My Lord lead me home
Please stay now with me, as I walk this world alone

But if I fall away, never further than today
It is for Your grace I pray, if I fall away

If I fall away

~ Canuel ~
34

Lord In Me

Lord I sing that You are mighty
Lord I sing of Your mercy, for me
Lord I sing that You are worthy
Lord I sing of Your mercy for me
Lord for me

Lord I sing of Your glory
Lord I sing of Your mercy, for me
Lord I sing of Your beauty
Lord I sing of Your mercy for me
Lord for me

And I sing of Your grace and Your love
Of Your everlasting love for me
And I sing of Your grace and Your faith
Of Your never ending faith in me, Lord in me
Your faith in me, Lord in me
Lord in me, Lord in me

Lord I sing that You are holy
Lord I sing of Your mercy for me
Lord I sing that You are
Lord I sing of Your mercy for me
Lord for me

And I sing of Your grace and Your love
Of Your everlasting love for me
And I sing of Your grace and Your faith
Of Your never ending faith in me, Lord in me
Your faith in me, Lord in me
Lord in me, Lord in me

~ Canuel ~
35

God Be Merciful

God be merciful
God be merciful to me
For my soul trusts in You
Under the shadow of Your wings
God be merciful
God be merciful, to me

God be merciful
God be merciful to me
For in Your arms I will rest
Until Your hands calm the sea
God be merciful
God be merciful, to me

And I will cry
Out to God most high
And I will cry
Out to God most high
Yes I will cry
Out to God most high

God be merciful
God be merciful, merciful to me

~ Canuel ~
36

Lord I Come

Lord I come, and here I kneel
I kneel now before You
Here before Your cross
Lord I come, and here I feel
I feel so alone, as I wander lost

Lord I come, to You this morning
So full of doubt, so full of fear
Lord ease my pain, it's all so unclear
Lord I come

Lord I pray, to You this morning
To hear my cries, to hear my hearts call
To bridge this distance, now as I crawl
Lord I come

Lord I come, and here I kneel
I kneel now before You
Here before Your cross
Lord I come, and here I feel
I feel so alone, as I wander lost
But Lord I come

Lord I cry, out to You this morning
To heal my hurt, heal this broken heart
To see through my lies, set my soul apart
Lord I come

Lord I come, and here I kneel
I kneel now before You
Here before Your cross
Lord I come, and here I feel
I feel so alone, as I wander lost
But Lord I come

Lord I come, to You this morning

~ Canuel ~
37

Nothing Remains

Take my heart, and free my soul
Take all you need from me

Take my sin, and make me whole
All you want me now to be

Take my life, and make it Yours
It is no longer mine to live

Take my doubt, and make me strong
All that I have left to give

For who I was
For who I was before
I am no longer now
Nothing remains
For where I walked
For where I walked before
I am no longer found
Nothing remains

Take my pain, and dry my tears
Get me through another day

Take my hand, and calm my fears
Here safe in Your keep I will stay

This is how I feel
I will not change my mind
Nothing could be more real
It will not fade away in time

Take my faith, and have it fly
Give me now the wings to soar

Take my soul, and change what's inside
Have me be now something more

For who I was
For who I was before
I am no longer now
Nothing remains
For where I walked
For where I walked before
I am no longer found
Nothing remains

~ Canuel ~

All of You

You've forgiven me, of all my sin
You've accepted me, of all I've been

Now I want to pray with You, stay with You
Hold on now to You
I want to walk with You, talk with You
Be now a part of, all of You, all of You

You've remembered me, in my times alone
You've invited me, into Your Heavenly home

Now I want to pray with You, stay with You
Hold on now to You
I want to walk with You, talk with You
Be now a part of, all of You, all of You

Lord because of Your endless love
My heart'll make it through the night
An' though the rain so hard it falls
Lord my heart, it will be alright
Lord my heart, it will be alright

Lord because of Your endless love
My soul now has wings to fly
An' though my tears so hard they fall
Lord my soul, it will be alright
Lord my soul, it will be alright

You've forgiven me, of all my sin
You've accepted me, of all I've been

~ Canuel ~
39

In Prayer

In prayer
I now kneel, before You Lord
And in prayer, I will pray

In hope
I now call, out to You Lord
And in hope, I will stay

In faith
I now kneel, before You Lord
And in faith, I will live

In song
I now sing, just for You Lord
And in a song, I will give

Now in faith
I'm here by You Lord
I'm here on my own accord
Lord I am here in faith

Now in faith
I come before Your throne
I come as one of Your own
Lord I come here in faith

Now in hope
I stand with my arms raised high
I stand not ashamed to cry
Lord I stand here in hope

So in prayer
I kneel at Your alter, to fall
I kneel only your name to call
Lord I kneel here in prayer

Lord I am here
In prayer

~ Canuel ~
40

Lord Reach Down

Lord reach down, and lift my soul
My Lord reach down, and make me whole
Lord reach down, and dry my tears
My Lord reach down, and calm my fears

And from where you are, Lord reach down!
And from where you are, my Lord reach down!

Lord reach down, and hold my heart
My Lord reach down, and set me apart
Lord reach down, and hear my prayers
My Lord reach down, and find me here

And from where you are, Lord reach down!
And from where you are, my Lord reach down!

I want to be where You are, no matter how far
I want to be there, Lord I want to be there
I want to be by Your side, no matter the divide
I want to be there, Lord I want to be there

So Lord reach down, and speak my name
My Lord reach down, and bear my blame
Lord reach down, and take me home
My Lord reach down, and make me Your own

And from where you are, my Lord reach down!
My Lord reach down!

~ Canuel ~
41

Because of My Faith

I have hope
In my desperate of times
I have a light
That in the darkness now shines

Because of faith
Because of my faith

I have strength
In my weakest of times
I have a love
That in my heart now shines

Because of faith
Because of my faith

Because of my faith
I have an eternal home
My heart it will never know
Another moment alone

Because of my faith
I have a forever love
My heart it will only ever know
Glory at Your throne

Because of faith
Because of my faith

~ Canuel ~
42

I'll Pray to The Lord

I'll pray to You Lord
To hold my broken heart
To kneel here beside me
Lord, hold my heart

I'll pray to You Lord
To live within my life
To remain ever close
Lord, live in my life

And I'll pray to You Lord
I'll wait upon You Lord
And I'll stay with You Lord
I will pray to You Lord

I'll pray to You Lord
To take away each tear
To wipe every one dry
Lord, take my tears

I'll pray to You Lord
To fight for my faith
To pray for my prayers
Lord, fight for my faith

And I'll pray to You Lord
I'll wait upon You Lord
And I'll stay with You Lord
I will pray to You Lord

I'll pray to You Lord
To seek my lost soul
To touch me now
Lord, seek my soul

I'll pray to You Lord
To sing with me this song
To now sing along
Lord, sing with me this song

And I'll pray to You Lord
I'll wait upon You Lord
And I'll stay with You Lord
I will pray to You Lord

~ Canuel ~
43

Only for Today

Lord I'll pray, for this day
For every trial, that I will go through

Lord I'll pray, just for today
For every step, that I will walk with You

Lord I'll pray, not for tomorrow
Not for yesterday
Not for what is to come, not for what has been
Lord I will pray, only for today

Lord I'll pray, for this day
For every tear, that I will cry in shame

Lord I'll pray, just for today
For every word, that I will speak in vain

Lord I'll pray, that Your will be done
To one day walk together, just as one

Lord I'll pray, that Your will be done
To one day walk with You
Along the streets of gold!

Lord I'll pray, for this day
For every time, that I will Your love forsake

Lord I'll pray, just for today
For every promise, that I will again break

Lord I'll pray, not for tomorrow
Not for yesterday
Not for what is to come, not for what has been
Lord I will pray, only for today

Only for today

~ Canuel ~
44

Do They See, You Lord in Me?

Do they see, You Lord in me?
Is Your love, the first gift I bring?
Do they see, You Lord in me?
Is Your love, the first song I sing?
For You

Lord now through Your eyes
Have me see the world
Just as You see the world
Through Your eyes

Lord now through Your grace
Have me love this world
Just as You love the world
Through Your grace

Do they see, You Lord in me?
Is Your love, the first word I speak?
Do they see, You Lord in me?
Is Your love, the first love I seek
For You

Do they see, You Lord in me?

~ Canuel ~
45

Echoes

Lord light my way
Be the lantern upon the approaching shore
I'm not afraid, not of the night
Nor of the impending dawn

For I am strong in my soul
I am steadfast within my faith
Now into the sea, my childish dreams
They've been cast away
Into the mist, and only the echoes now remains
Into the mist, only the echoes now remains

Lord once upon the shore
You'll be the rock that I shall anchor to
As I walk this road, keep my path narrow
Through the trials that I pass through

It takes faith, to walk alone through this world
To stand firm, hard against the wind
It takes deep faith, to believe within the blood
That washes away my every sin

As I walk this world
You whisper prayers into these learning ears
I'm no longer blind
I witness truth, through these burning tears

For I am strong in my soul
I am steadfast within my faith
Now into the sea, my childish dreams
They've been cast away
Into the mist, and only the echoes now remains
Into the mist, only the echoes now remains

~ Canuel ~
46

Here on My Knees

Oh Lord when I pray
Have me pray here on my knees
Oh Lord have me pray

Oh Lord when I cry
Have me cry here on my knees
Oh Lord have me cry

Because when I am here on my knees
With my eyes now lifted high
I know my eyes, are now upon You

Because when I am here on my knees
Within my heart, my hopes they rise
And I know my heart, is now with You

Oh Lord when I fall
Have me fall here on my knees
Oh Lord have me fall

Oh Lord when I stay
Have me stay here on my knees
Oh Lord have me stay

Because when I am here on my knees
With my eyes now lifted high
I know my eyes, are now upon You

Because when I am here on my knees
Within my heart, my hopes they rise
And I know my heart, is now with You

Oh Lord as I believe
Have me believe, here on my knees
Oh Lord, have me believe
Here on my knees

~ Canuel ~
47

This Confession

I kneel before your alter
My every sin I now bring

And I pray I'll never falter
My every tear, how it now stings

I feel so much is unspoken
By every word I now use

I've made each promise I've broken
By every lie by which I now choose

Oh Lord, these tears I cry that fall
Oh Lord these prayers
That I pray, I call, to you
It's what is hidden within my soul
Is what I need to know
In this confession of my soul

I sense that I'm now clearing
Every thought that's littered this mind

I feel that I'm now nearing
Every path I'd always hoped to find

I kneel before your alter
My every sin I now bring

I pray I'll never falter
My every tear, how it now stings

Oh Lord, these tears I cry that fall
Oh Lord these prayers
That I pray, I call, to you
It's what is hidden within my soul
Is what I need to know
In this confession of my soul

~ Canuel ~
48

So Now Arise

In my place He stood there strong
He left no trace for sin to belong

Yet here I stand I'm so full of shame
For on my own this stain can only remain

In my place He stood there alone
Upon His face my scars as yet unknown

Yet here I fall time and again
So I reach out to You once again my Friend

So now arise, and stand aside of me
Be not surprised by what your eyes will see
So now arise, and walk here with me
Be not surprised by what your faith can be

In my place He stood there at home
This heart He embraced and rolled away its heavy stone

Yet here I sin so alone I will fall
Will my soul ever listen to the invitation of Your spirits call?

He recites every promise
That He intends to keep
Whispers every name
In the tears that He weeps

He remembers every moment
That will ever be
He kooks deep within the eyes
That the world will never see

In my place He stood there to atone
My every sin retraced by this one perfect soul

Yet here I kneel humble a the foot of your cross
Am I to just to wander as another life lost?

So now arise, and stand aside of me
Be not surprised by what your eyes will see
So now arise, and walk here with me
Be not surprised by what your faith can be
So now arise!

~ Canuel ~
49

I've Made My Choice

Lord I'll go, where You want me to go
Lord I will stay, where You want me to stay
Lord I'll follow, just as You want me to follow

Lord I'll leave, when You want me to leave
Lord I will wait, when You want me to wait
Lord I'll lead, just as You want me to lead

Whatever of me that You choose
Whatever of me that You use
Lord I will hear, I listen to Your voice

Whatever of me that You need
Whatever of me that You free
Lord I will live, I have made my choice

Lord I'll learn, what You want me to learn
Lord I will pray, what You want me to pray
Lord I'll be silent, just as You want me to be silent

Lord I'll be, all You want me to be
Lord I will say, all You want me to say
Lord I'll praise, just as You want me to praise

To be closer
Ever closer to your side
To be nearer
Ever nearer to your side

Lord I'll go, where You want me to go
Lord I will stay, where You want me to stay
Lord I'll follow, just as You want me to follow
I have made my choice

~ Canuel ~
50

3

By Faith Alone

By Faith Alone

My salvation
It is by grace alone
Not by my works, not by what I can do
But by grace alone
By grace alone

My salvation
It is by faith alone
Not by my words, not by what I can prove
But by faith alone
By faith alone

For faith alone, brings me here
Before Your throne
For faith alone, blesses me to hear
Your voice calling me home
By faith alone

Nothing on my own
Here all alone, will earn my way
Nothing I can see
Here in front of me, will change the faith I feel today

My salvation
It is by grace alone

My salvation
It is by faith alone

By faith alone

~ Canuel ~
51

Closer

Lord as I now step, out into this faith
Bless me with the strength I'll need today

Lord as I now walk close, closer now to You
Whisper now to me, Your words to pray

**Lord have me live Your will
Have my soul be still
Lord keep me closer to Your love**

**Have me keep an open heart
May our paths never part
Lord keep me closer to Your love**

Lord I fear this fear, I fear right now
Fill me with Your love, and hold me near

Lord as I stand close, closer now to You
Whisper now to me, this one prayer

*Closer now to Your cross
Closer now to Your truth
Lord keep me closer, to Your love*

*Closer now to Your heart
Closer now to Your words
Lord keep me closer
Lord keep me closer
Lord keep me closer, to Your love*

**Lord have me live Your will
Have my soul be still
Lord keep me closer to Your love**

**Have me keep an open heart
May our paths never part
Lord keep me closer to Your love**

Closer

~ Canuel ~
52

Come To Me

Come to me, all who have been broken
And I will heal your heart

Come to me, all who have cried
And I will dry your tears
I will dry your tears

Come to me, all who have been silent
And I will sing you a new song

Come to me, all who have hurt
And I will ease your pain
I will ease your pain

Come to Me
Come to My side
Come to My cross
Come to my open arms
Come to Me

Come to me, all who have been lost
And I will find your way home

Come to me, all who have given up
And I will be your strength, Yes I will be your strength

To all who have fallen
I will lift you up
To all who have been afraid
I will give you hope

To all have been blind
I will help you see
And to all who doubt
I will show you your faith

Come to Me
Come to My side
Come to My cross
Come to my open arms
Come to Me

~ *Canuel* ~
53

When Morning Comes

When morning comes
All your tears will dry
No longer will you have, the need to cry
When morning comes

When morning comes,
All your fears will fade
No longer will you have, to be afraid
When morning comes

And You will find, your lost smile again
You will find all of your faith again
When morning comes

When morning comes
All your sorrow will end
No longer will you have, to feel this alone again
When morning comes

And You will find, your lost smile again
You will find all of your faith again
When morning comes

When morning comes
All of your hurt will heal
No longer will you have, to feel this pain you feel
When morning comes

And You will find, your lost smile again
You will find all of your faith again
When morning comes

~ Canuel ~
54

Lord of All

Lord of all, send me Your grace
To this heart, this soul, this place

Lord of all, send me Your light
To this heart, to this soul tonight
Lord of all, please send me Your light

Lord of all, send me Your love
To this heart, this soul now from above

Lord of all, send me Your prayer
To this heart, this soul lost out here
Lord of all, please send me Your prayer

Send me Your saving rain
To wash away my pain
Send me Your saving rain
To wash away my tears
Lord send me Your saving rain

Lord of all, send me Your word
To this heart, so this soul it may learn

Lord of all, send me Your song
To this heart, so this soul may sing along
Lord of all, please send me Your song

Lord of all, please send me Your grace
Lord of all, please send me Your light
Lord of all, please send me Your love

Lord of all, please send me Your prayer
Lord of all, please send me Your word
Lord of all, please send me Your song
Lord of all

~ Canuel ~
55

To The One

To the One, who laid down His life
I now offer up my soul!

To the One, who spoke to me truth
I now sing this song of love!

**Of my humbleness, my willingness
I seek Your deliverance, for my faithlessness**

To the One, who reached to this earth
I now lift my heart in praise!

To the One, who bore the guilt of my sin
I now glorify Your name!

**Lord awake my awareness
As I stand here defenseless
I will walk in Your presence
Be remade in Your likeness
I will be Your witness
And breathe in Your brilliance
For I am here now speechless
Have me still in my silence**

To the One

**I now ask Your forgiveness
For being so careless
I now see through my blindness
I'm before You now breathless**

To the One, who was covered in my shame
I now bow my head in prayer!
To the One

~ Canuel ~
56

Beneath Your Cross

Beneath Your cross
Here I kneel
Your gift is to my soul
My soul to heal

Deep into Your eyes
Through my tears I stare
Lord make my life
For You a prayer

Beneath Your cross
All I bring
Here You hold my heart
To this soul You sing

For I have peace
Found a perfect peace
Lord prepare a place
At Your table of feast

Beneath Your cross
Here I kneel
The pain of the truth
My soul it now feels

Deep into Your eyes
Through my tears I stare
Lord, the love of Your cross
My heart's to share
Beneath Your cross

~ Canuel ~
57

It's a Matter of Faith

It's a matter of faith
A matter of an endless love
It's a matter of intention

It's a matter of mercy
A matter of a healing grace
It's a matter of dedication

It's a matter of faith

It's a matter of hope
A matter of His Holy word
It's a matter of perception

It's a matter of a prayer
A matter of kneeling down
It's a matter of conviction

It's a matter of hope

It's a matter of a cross
A matter of His flowing blood
It's a matter of devotion

It's a matter of joy
A matter of an eternal life
It's a matter of salvation

It's a matter of a cross
It's a matter of hope
It's a matter of faith

~ Canuel ~
58

At This Cross

At this cross I kneel
At this cross my hurt is healed
At this cross what love I feel
At this cross I kneel

At this cross I cry
At this cross my tears are dried
At this cross what joy I find
At this cross I cry

No where else
No other way
No other place
But here at this cross
At this cross

At this cross I pray
At this cross my soul is saved
At this cross what a price was paid
At this cross I pray

At this cross I fall
At this cross my heart it calls
At this cross I give You all
At this cross I fall

No where else
No other way
No other place
But here at this cross
At this cross

~ Canuel ~
59

In The Shadow of Your Wings

In the shadow of Your wings
I will find my rest
Lord my soul will be blessed

In the shadow of Your wings
I will lift my praise
Lord I'll know Your grace
In the shadow of Your wings

**And my heart will cry
Out to God most high
And my voice will sing
Gifts of love I'll bring**

**And my eyes will see
Your glory and majesty
Of You alone my King
In the shadow of Your wings**

*In the shadow of Your wings
I will here bow down
Lord here I'll cast my crowns*

*In the shadow of Your wings
I will forever pray
Lord I will forever stay
In the shadow of Your wings*

**And my heart will cry
Out to God most high
And my voice will sing
Gifts of love I'll bring**

**And my eyes will see
Your glory and majesty
Of You alone my King
In the shadow of Your wings**

~ Canuel ~
60

Only You Lord

Only You Lord, reach out Your hand
Draw me nearer, to where You stand

Only You Lord, speak now the truth
Make it clearer, my point of view

Only You Lord, died for me
To bring me closer, to set this soul free
Only You Lord, will come again
To take me higher, with You my friend
Take me higher, with You my friend

Only You Lord, my heart You hold
I watch with wonder, my life unfold

Only You Lord, for this soul came
My deliverer, You whisper my name

Only You Lord, died for me
To bring me closer, to set this soul free
Only You Lord, will come again
To take me higher, with You my friend
Take me higher, with You my friend

Only You Lord, reach out Your hand
Draw me nearer, to where You stand

Only You Lord, died for me
To bring me closer, to set this soul free

~ Canuel ~

61

Your Dear Love

Even if I now took this time now to pray
Dear Lord what in the world would you want me to say?

Would I dare ask of You, "Oh Lord forgive me please?"
Would You find me here kneeling, down upon my knees?

Oh Lord I have never been, anywhere near here before
I've never tried to turn this key, and walk through this door

I've never felt these tears, fall like this before
Oh Lord I've never needed, Your dear love anymore

So even if I don't deserve to be here now with You
Oh Lord please don't turn me away and You have every right to

Should I speak of all I have or all I have not done?
Or should I just walk away, can we share one moment alone?

Oh Lord I have never been, anywhere near here before
I've never tried to turn this key, and walk through this door

I've never felt these tears, fall like this before
Oh Lord I've never needed, Your dear love anymore

With my every step taken, sometimes I feel further away
With my every whisper spoken, do you not hear what I say?

My heart it has been shaken, yet I'm here to try again
With another promise broken, with another bridge to mend

Even if I took this time now to stay
Oh Lord it is my own heart, I fear that might tear me away

Could I still fall away, will You find me once again?
Could I still call to you and You listen to my heart as a friend?

Oh Lord I have never been, anywhere near here before
I've never tried to turn this key, and walk through this door

I've never felt these tears, fall like this before
Oh Lord I've never needed, Your dear love anymore

~ Canuel ~

One

We are of one faith, we are of one church
We are just one gathering

We are of one hope, we are of one love
We are just one worshiping, one!

We are of one soul, we are of one truth
We are just one family

We are of one heart, we are of one word
We are just one faithfully, one!

We are one!
Never to be divided
Never to be separated, one!

We are one!
Always to remain together
Always to remain forever, one!

We are of one grace, we are of one cross
We are just one joyfully

We are of one King, we are of one Lord
We are just one eternally, one!

We are one!
Never to be divided
Never to be separated, one!

We are one!
Always to remain together
Always to remain forever, one!

We are one, just one mercy
One glory, just one salvation!
We are one, just one savior
One redeemer, just one creation, one!

We are of one voice, we are of one God
We're just one prayerfully, one!

~ Canuel ~

Ever Closer

Through our every prayer
Here deep within our faith

Through our every song
Here deep within our praise

**We grow, ever stronger
We grow, ever closer**

Through every joyful tear
Felt here, deep within Your grace

Through each burden that we share
Found here, deep within this place

**We grow, ever stronger
We grow, ever closer**

~ Canuel ~
64

Let It Fall

Lord may Your glory shine down
All around me now
Lord may Your glory shine down

Lord may Your mercy shine down
All around me now
Lord may Your mercy shine down

Lord may it fall now surround me
Lord may it fall, all around me now
Lord let it fall!

Lord may Your hope shine down
All around me now
Lord may Your hope shine down

Lord may Your love shine down
All around me now
Lord may Your love shine down

Lord may it fall now surround me
Lord may it fall, all around me now
Lord let it fall!

Let it fall like the rain
Washing away all of my shame
Let it fall like the rain
Washing away all of my blame
Lord let it fall
Let it fall!

Lord may Your grace shine down
All around me now
Lord may Your grace shine down

Lord may Your peace shine down
All around me now
Lord may Your peace shine down

Lord may it fall now surround me
Lord may it fall, all around me now
Lord let it fall!

~ Canuel ~
65

Just Open Your Eyes

There is love, in the heart of the Lord
An' there you'll find, you will find love
Yes there is hope, in the grace of the Lord
An' there you'll find, you will find hope

There is peace, in the prayers of the Lord
An' there you'll find, you will find peace
Yes there is strength, in the arms of the Lord
An' there you'll find, you will find strength

Just seek and you shall find
For you are no longer blind
Just open up, open your eyes

There is joy, in the name of the Lord
An' there you'll find, you will find joy
Yes there is life, in the cross, of the Lord
An' there you'll find, you will find life

Just seek and you shall find
For you are no longer blind
Just open up, open your eyes

There is truth, in the words, of the Lord
An' there you'll find, you will find truth
There is praise, in the song of the Lord
An' there you'll find, you will find praise

Just seek and you shall find
For you are no longer blind
Just open up, open your eyes

~ Canuel ~

All That Come

All that come
All will come to believe
All will bow at Your majesty

All that come, will be embraced
All will awaken, come face to face
All will awaken, come face to face

All that come
All in praise will sing
All will join the choir, of our Lord and King

All that come, all will be blessed
All will shake off the dust that this world has left
All will shake off the dust this world has left

All that come, all will rejoice
All will stand together now as one voice

All that come, all will delight
All will feel the warmth, of love's pure light
All will feel the warmth, of love's pure light

All will rest, gather in prayer
All will have hands to hold
A Friends love to share
All will cry, but only with their joyful tears
All tears will be wiped away, by Heavens Holy Heir

All that come, yes all hearts will praise
All will lift up in glory, all our faith can raise

All that come, yes all blind eyes will see
All will walk alone with Jesus, eternally
All will walk alone with Jesus, eternally

All that come
All will come to believe!

~ Canuel ~
67

Unseen

My every word, every prayer
Every sin, every tear

My every hope, every dream
Every moment, every scene

Lord I lay them all now before You
As broken pieces at Your feet
Lord I offer them all now to You
Together with all that remains unseen

My every loss, every gain
Every fear, every pain

My every hurt, every lie
Every lust, every cry

One by one, they are answered
One by one, they are sealed
One by one, they are heard
One by one, they are healed

My every joy, every breath
Every smile, Lord everything that is left!

Lord I lay them all now before You
As broken pieces at Your feet
Lord I offer them all now to You
Together with all that remains unseen
Unseen

~ Canuel ~
68

My First Love

Come back into my life Jesus
Come home again
My first love

Come back into my heart Jesus
Come home my friend
My first love

Take Your place
At the head of the table
We'll celebrate at Your return

Take Your place
Here at my table
We'll rejoice at Your return

You've been gone, for far too long
I don't want You to ever go away again
Never again!

Come back into my arms Jesus
Come home to stay
My first love

Come back into my faith Jesus
Come home to pray
My first love

Take Your place
At the head of the table
We'll celebrate at Your return

Take Your place
Here at my table
We'll rejoice at Your return

So come back into my life Jesus
Come home again
My first love

~ Canuel ~
69

The Wings of Love

Through the darkest of my days, a ray of light appears
Like a song of the Angels, like thunder in my ears

And it opens my blind eyes, to see the clouds of white
And whispers Heaven's gates, are now open wide

And I believe that my Savior, He is alive
And it's for my sin, that He laid down his life

I will live and so breathe, the words that He said
"Take up My cross and walk in My way"

And I pledge my life, to the Lamb on the cross
During my life's every gain, my life's every loss

For my soul can now fly, as the wings of the dove
And my soul will fly, on the wings, on the wings of love

To be saved of my sin, is it just to believe?
Such easy words to follow, yet quite another to live

To lay down ones life, your soul for the Lord
To shoulder His cross, to carry His sword

And believe that your savior, He is alive
And it's for your sin, that He laid down His life

So live and so breathe, the words that He said
"Take up My cross and walk in My way"

I believe in the prayers, that He prayed in the upper room
In His resurrection, in His empty tomb

That He raised Lazarus, dead four days in his grave
He bore the weight of the world, it was my life to save

I will pledge my life, to the Lamb on the cross
During my life's every gain, my life's every loss

For my soul can now fly, as the wings of the dove
And my soul will fly, on the wings, on the wings of love

~ Canuel ~
70

Today Is The Day

Today is the day
That I'm gonna sing of my praise
Today is the day
That I'm gonna lift up Your name
And I'm gonna sing of my praise
And I'm gonna lift up Your name

Today is the day
That I'm gonna cry out in my faith
Today is the day
That I'm gonna pray for Your grace
And I'm gonna cry out in my faith
And I'm gonna pray for Your grace

This is the day
That I've been waiting for, all of my life

Today is the day
That I'm gonna live within Your love
Today is the day
That I'm gonna look to You above
And I'm gonna live within Your love
And I'm gonna look to You above

This is the day
That I've been waiting for, all of my life

Today is the day
That 'm gonna count all my gain as loss
Today is the day
That I'm gonna fall down here at Your cross
And I'm gonna count all my gain as loss
And I'm gonna fall down at Your cross

This is the day
That I've been waiting for, all of my life

~ Canuel ~

As One Church

As one church
Now Lord we stand
To lift high Your name
All across this land

As one church
Now Lord we sing
To You our God
Friend, Savior, King

As one church
Now Lord we pray
To now touch our hearts
For You to bless this day

As one church
Now Lord we cry
To remain at Your cross
Remain by Your side

As one church
Now Lord we praise
To serve You in love
To walk in Your grace

As one church
Now Lord we believe
That throughout our faith
Our blind eyes they will see

As one church
Now Lord we're gathered here
Forever keep us close
Heaven hold us near
As one church

~ Canuel ~
72

Far Away

Lord I want to be forever with You
I want to be just where You are
Lord I want to be together with You
I want to be just where You are

I don't want to be too far away
Stand by your side both night and day
I don't want to be too far away
Rest in Your arms is what I pray
I don't want to be too far away

Lord I want to pray now with You
I want to be just where You are
Lord I want to stay now with You
I want to be just where You are

I don't want to be too far away
Stand by your side both night and day
I don't want to be too far away
Rest in Your arms is what I pray
I don't want to be too far away

Lord I want to walk nearer to You
I want to be just where You are
Lord I want to draw closer to You
I want to be just where You are

I don't want to be too far away
Stand by your side both night and day
I don't want to be too far away
Rest in Your arms is what I pray
I don't want to be too far away

~ Canuel ~
73

Was It You?

Was it You?
Who whispered my name
High above the roar

Was it You?
Who bore all of my blame
For all that I've done wrong

Lord was it You?

Was it You?
Who loosened these chains
And set my lost soul free

Was it You?
Who began this change
Here deep inside of me

Lord was it You?

**Lord You've opened my heart
So that I would believe?
Lord You've opened my eyes
So that I would see**

Lord was it You?

~Canuel~
74

The Winds

Have the winds overtake this heart
Have the rains wash away my doubt

Have my life receive its second birth
And I will sing to the ends of the earth!

Have this faith drive back my fears
Have Your love wipe away my tears

Have my eyes look to Your eyes first
And I will sing to the ends of the earth!

From the first light of this day
To the very last dream now of the night
From the first star of this sky
To the very last moment I'm alive

Oh Lord, my life will honor You
Oh Lord, my life will honor You

Have Your trumpet roll back the clouds
Have Your choir now sing out loud

Have Your hope fill this soul's thirst
And I will sing to the ends of the earth!

From the first light of this day
To the very last dream now of the night
From the first star of this sky
To the very last moment I'm alive

Have my life receive its second birth
And I will sing to the ends of the earth!

~ Canuel ~
75

4

I'll Praise The Lord

I'll Praise The Lord

I'll praise the Lord
With all of my soul
With all that is now within me

I'll praise the Lord
With all of my heart
With all that is now within me

**Oh Lord my God
My heavenly King
Find me on my knees
Let my praises ring
Oh Lord my God**

I'll praise the Lord
With all of my prayers
With all that is now within me

I'll praise the Lord
With all of my life
With all that is now within me

**Oh Lord my God
My heavenly King
Find me on my knees
Let my praises ring
Oh Lord my God**

I'll praise the Lord
With of all my soul
With all that is now within me
I'll praise the Lord

~ Canuel ~
76

Raise My Soul

Lord I feel so lonely
Though this world surrounds me
Lord I feel so all alone

Lord I feel so far away
Though I stand by Your side and pray
Lord I feel so far from home

Take my hand
Lift me up, from where I fall
Take my heart
Raise me up, Lord raise my soul
Raise my soul!

Lord I feel so empty
Though your arms reach to hold me
Lord I feel I'm on my own

Lord I feel You touch me
Though my heart it's aching
Lord I feel you're here, all along

Take my hand
Lift me up, from where I fall
Take my heart
Raise me up, Lord raise my soul
Raise my soul!

Lord I feel, you raise my soul
Raise my soul

~ Canuel ~
77

There Is A Savior

There is a Savior who will save
He'll give His hope to the hopeless

There is a Savior who will save
He'll give His faith to the faithless

There is a Savior who will save
He'll give His light to the darkness

There is a Savior who will save
He'll give His grace and forgiveness

He will give us His hope
His hope to the hopeless

He will give us His faith
His faith to the faithless

He will give us His light
His light to the darkness

He will give us His grace
His grace and forgiveness

There is a Savior who will save

~ Canuel ~
78

Jesus Holy One

Long, is the road ahead
And dark, is the night to come
But Lord in faith I will follow
Yes I will follow where You've led
Jesus Holy One

Hard, will be the fight
And we will dance when the day is done
But Lord in hope I'll stand by You
Yes I will stand right by Your side
Jesus Holy One

Jesus Holy One
I will praise Your name
Jesus Holy One
I will praise Your name
Jesus Holy One

And love, it will be our song
And we will sing forevermore
But Lord in love I will praise You
Yes I'll praise You alone
Jesus Holy One

Jesus Holy One
I will praise Your name
Jesus Holy One
I will praise Your name
Jesus Holy One

~ Canuel ~
79

On The Third Day

On the third day, at early dawn
They gathered together in their room
And on the third day, as they prayed alone
They lifted praise unto the Lord

**And they prayed, Halleluiah, Halleluiah, Halleluiah
He is the Lord our God
And they prayed, Halleluiah, Halleluiah, Halleluiah
He is the Lord, the Lord our God**

On the third day, with gifts in hand
They walked the road towards the tomb
And on the third day, as they drew near
They found the stone had been moved

**And they sang, Halleluiah, Halleluiah, Halleluiah
He's rolled away the stone
And they sang, Halleluiah, Halleluiah, Halleluiah
He's rolled away, away the stone**

On the third day, they entered in
He'd risen just as He had said
And on the third day, the angel spoke
"Why do you seek the living among the dead?"

**So sing, Halleluiah, Halleluiah, Halleluiah
Praise the Lord He arose
So sing, Halleluiah, Halleluiah, Halleluiah
Praise the Lord He arose
So sing, Halleluiah, Halleluiah, Halleluiah
He is the Lord our God
And they sang, Halleluiah, Halleluiah, Halleluiah
He's rolled away, away the stone**

~ Canuel ~
80

All Across The Sky

I can feel His love, now inside of me
I can feel His grace, now forgiving me
I can feel the love, of the Lord deep within me

I can feel His hope, now surrounding me
I can feel His strength, now protecting me
I can feel the love, of the Lord deep within me
So deep within me

Lord You've given me the wings, the wings now to fly
And I will write Your name, all across the sky
Lord I'll write Your name, all across the sky

I can feel His truth, now defending me
I can feel His faith, now believing in me
I can feel the love, of the Lord deep within me
So deep within me

Lord You've given me the wings, the wings now to fly
And I will write Your name, all across the sky
Lord I'll write Your name, all across the sky

I can feel His prayers, now restoring me
I can feel His joy, now rising up in me
I can feel the love, of the Lord deep within me
So deep within me, so deep within me

Lord You've given me the wings, the wings now to fly
And I will write Your name, all across the sky
Lord I'll write Your name, all across the sky

Lord I'll write Your name, all across the sky

I can feel the love, of the Lord deep within me
So deep within me, so deep within me

~ Canuel ~
81

Sing!

When you feel praise
Come on and sing a song to the Lord
When you feel love
Come on and sing your song to the Lord
Sing a song to the Lord,
Sing Your song to the Lord

Sing your song
Come on and sing Your song to the Lord
Sing Your song to the Lord

When you feel faith
Come on and sing a song to the Lord
When you feel grace
Come on and sing Your song to the Lord
Sing a song to the Lord
Sing Your song to the Lord

Sing your song
Come on and sing Your song to the Lord
Sing Your song to the Lord!

~ Canuel ~
82

Forgiven

Lord by Your mercy, I'm forgiven
Lord by Your grace, I am redeemed
Lord by Your hand, I'm delivered
Lord by Your blood, I am washed clean
I'm washed clean

Lord nothing I can do
Here on my own, can my works change
Lord nothing I can say
Here all alone, can my words change
Lord can I change, Lord can I change

Lord by Your love, I am ransomed
Lord by Your faith, I'm all that I can be
Lord by Your word, I'm spoken for
Lord by Your truth, I am set free
I'm set free

Lord nothing I can do
Here on my own, can my works change
Lord nothing I can say
Here all alone, can my words change
Lord can I change, Lord can I change

Lord by Your mercy, I'm forgiven
Lord by Your grace, I am redeemed
Lord by Your hand, I'm delivered
Lord by Your blood, I am washed clean
I'm washed clean

~ Canuel ~
83

Deep In My Soul

I want to show you
Just what my soul believes
Yes I want to show you
Just what my eyes now see

An' tell you,
Just what I feel, here in my heart
Just what I know, deep in my soul
Just what I feel, here in my heart
Just what I know, deep in my soul

I want to find you
No matter where you are
Yes I want to find you
No matter just how far

An' tell you,
Just what I feel, here in my heart
Just what I know, deep in my soul
Just what I feel, here in my heart
Just what I know, deep in my soul

I want to hold you
So you'll never feel alone
Yes I want to hold you
So you'll always feel at home, right at home
I want to tell you, I want to tell you

An' tell you,
Just what I feel, here in my heart
Just what I know, deep in my soul
Just what I feel, here in my heart
Just what I know, deep in my soul

I want to show you, I want to find you

An' tell you,
Just what I feel, here in my heart
Just what I know, deep in my soul
Just what I feel, here in my heart
Just what I know, deep in my soul

~ Canuel ~
84

Every Step of the Way

Through all of the storms, all of the rain
Through all of the hurt, all of the pain
My Lord You walk with me, every step of the way

Through all of the doubt, all of the faith
Through all of the love, all of the hate
My Lord You walk with me, every step of the way

Lord You are the hand which I hold
You are my guide as I grow old
Lord You are the hope of my heart
Lord You are the name which I speak
You are my strength as I am weak
Lord You are the hope, of my heart

Through all of day, all of the night
Through all of the wrong, all of the right
My Lord You walk with me, every step of the way

Lord You are the hand which I hold
You are my guide as I grow old
Lord You are the hope of my heart
Lord You are the name which I speak
You are my strength as I am weak
Lord You are the hope, of my heart

My Lord You walk with me, every step of the way

~ Canuel ~
85

There's Such Beauty Here

There's such beauty here
My eyes look everywhere
Into every corner of the world

There's such beauty here
I cannot help but stare
Into the eyes of this one little girl

How can I tell you, I love you?
Just how perfect you are
How can I tell you, I love you?
Just how beautiful you are
Just how perfect you are

There's such beauty here
If more I know not where
I just look now up at the stars

There's such beauty here
Blink an' it may just disappear
To touch heaven now isn't so far

How can I tell you, I love you?
Just how precious you are
How can I tell you, I love you?
Just how wonderful you are
Just how precious you are

There's such beauty here
Yet it cannot now compare
As to the depths of our love

There's such beauty here
Life has never been more clear
As this endless blue sky above

How can I tell you, I love you?
Just how special you are
How can I tell you, I love you?
Just how amazing you are
Just how special you are

There's such beauty here
My eyes look everywhere
Into every corner of the world

~ Canuel ~
86

Come To My Altar

Come to my altar
All who are broken
And I will heal your heart

Come to my altar
All who are crying
And I will dry your tears

Come to my altar
All who are silent
And I will sing you a new song

Come to my alter
All who are hurting
And I will ease all your pain

Come to my altar
All who are weary
And I will be your strength

Come to my altar
All who are searching
And I'll find your way home

**To have fallen
I will lift you up
To all who have been afraid
I will give to you hope
To all that have been so blind
I will help you see
And to all who have ever doubted
I will give to you faith**

Come to my altar
All who are broken
And I will heal your heart

I will heal your heart

~ Canuel ~
87

All Because Of You

Some may say, that I'm saved
That I've found my forgiveness and my grace
It's all because of You, it's all because of You

Some may say, that I've changed
That nothing about me is the same
It's all because of You, it's all because of You

From where there was doubt, now there is faith
From where there was sin, now there is strength
And now all that I do, yes now all that I do
It's all because of You

Well some may say, that I'm blessed
That now in Your loving arms is where I rest
It's all because of You, it's all because of You

Still some may say, that I am free
That by faith my soul, it now believes
It's all because of You, it's all because of You

From where there was doubt, now there is faith
From where there was sin, now there is strength
And now all that I do, yes now all that I do
It's all because of You

Some may say, that I'm saved
That I've found my forgiveness and my grace
It's all because of You Lord, it's all because of You

From where there was doubt, now there is faith
From where there was sin, now there is strength
And now all that I do, yes now all that I do
It's all because of You

~ Canuel ~
88

My Jesus

My Jesus, my savior
My Jesus, my redeemer
My Jesus, my Jesus, my Lord
You are my Lord

My Jesus, my master
My Jesus, my deliverer
My Jesus, my Jesus, my God
You are my God

Lord You are my amazing grace
Lord You are my, star of the morning
Lord You are my endless strength
My hope, my everlasting

My Jesus, my healer
My Jesus, my forgiver
My Jesus, my Jesus, my Friend
You are my Friend

Lord You are my amazing grace
Lord You are my, star of the morning
Lord You are my endless strength
My hope, my everlasting

My Jesus, my teacher
My Jesus, my defender
My Jesus, my Jesus, my King
You are my King

Lord You are my amazing grace
Lord You are my, star of the morning
Lord You are my endless strength
My hope, my everlasting

My Jesus, my shelter
My Jesus, my protector
My Jesus, my Jesus, my Hope
You are my hope

Lord You are my amazing grace
Lord You are my, star of the morning
Lord You are my endless strength
My hope, my everlasting

Lord You are my hope...

~ Canuel ~
89

The Passion

With every drop of blood
That You shed for me
With every tear You cried
Each one that has set me free

**With every bead of sweat
That fell upon dirty ground
With every eye that Your eyes met
As You searched the crowd**

With every insult thrown
Screamed out in Your name
With every vacant stare
My Lord You bore that blame

**With every lash Your back felt
Never once in pain to cry out
With every step that Your feet walked
Such hate heard in every shout**

With every breath of dust
Life into this life You breathe
With every hit of the hammer hard
That Your gentle hands received

**With every sigh Your Mother sighed
Falling down, there at Your feet
With every prayer Your Father prayed
For it is now, that Your eyes meet**

With every drop of blood
That You shed for me
With every tear You cried
Each one that has set me free

~ Canuel ~
90

Jesus Christ!

Maybe you've taken for granted, maybe your whole life
Maybe it's your job, your home, or maybe your own wife

Maybe I'm here to tell you, that it's not too late
Maybe I'm here to show you His way

It's the Lord, Jesus Christ!
He is the way, the truth
The hope, He is the life!
It's the Lord, Jesus Christ!
He is the rock, the prayer
The path, He is the light!
It is the Lord, Jesus Christ!

Maybe you've awakened to, maybe no one's there
Maybe on your own alone, maybe life's not fair

Maybe I'm here to find you, hold out a hand to hold
Maybe this hand to hold, it's just in time

It's the Lord, Jesus Christ!
He is the way, the truth
The hope, He is the life!
It's the Lord, Jesus Christ!
He is the rock, the prayer
The path, He is the light!
It is the Lord, Jesus Christ!

Maybe it has taken you, maybe now all your time
Maybe you've remained too long, standing here in line

Maybe I'm here to invite you, to open up your eyes
Maybe to wipe the tears, just as you cry

It's the Lord, Jesus Christ!
He is the way, the truth
The hope, He is the life!
It's the Lord, Jesus Christ!
He is the rock, the prayer
The path, He is the light!
It is the Lord, Jesus Christ!

~ Canuel ~

I Will Praise

I will praise, Lord I will praise Your name
High above all other names
And Lord I will praise
Lord I will praise Your name
Your holy name

And I will praise
I will praise Your holy name

And I will sing, Lord I will sing Your name
High above all other names
And Lord I will sing
Lord I will sing Your name
Your holy name

And I will praise
I will praise Your holy name

I will cry, Lord I will cry Your name
High above all other names
And Lord I will cry
Lord I will cry Your name
Your holy name

And I will praise
I will praise Your holy name

I will shout, Lord I will shout Your name
High above all other names
And Lord I will shout
Lord I will shout Your name
Your holy name

And I will praise
I will praise Your holy name

I will praise Your holy name!

~ Canuel ~
92

My Lord Lives

My Lord lives here in my soul
My Lord's grace is my forgiveness, and my hope
My Lord lives!

My Lord lives here in my heart
My Lord's love is my beginning, and my start
My Lord lives!

My Lord lives here deep inside of me
Wide open now for all the world to see
For I am not who I used to be, I have changed
My Lord lives!

My Lord lives here in my life
My Lord's truth is my everything, and my light
My Lord lives!

My Lord lives here deep inside of me
Wide open now for all the world to see
For I am not who I used to be, I have changed
My Lord lives!

My Lord lives here in my faith
My Lord's cross is my salvation, and my strength
My Lord lives!

My Lord lives here deep inside of me
Wide open now for all the world to see
For I am not who I used to be, I have changed
My Lord lives!

~ Canuel ~
93

Stains

Oh Lord Your love, it's all I'll ever need
Oh Lord Your hope, it is my reason, to believe

Lord I hear, You whisper my name
Lord I offer, You all of my shame
Lord wash these sinful stains, from my hands

Oh Lord Your truth, it's all I'll ever want
Oh Lord Your grace, it is my reason, to carry on

Lord I hear, You whisper my name
Lord I offer, You all of my shame
Lord wash these sinful stains, from my hands

Oh Lord Your faith, it's all I'll ever seek
Oh Lord Your cross, it is my reason, now to be

Lord I hear, You whisper my name
Lord I offer, You all of my shame
Lord wash these sinful stains, from my hands

Oh Lord Your love, it's all I'll ever need
Oh Lord Your hope, it is my reason, to believe

Lord I hear, You whisper my name
Lord I offer, You all of my shame
Lord wash these sinful stains, from my hands

~ Canuel ~
94

Lord It's You

Lord it's You that I love
Lord it's You that I follow
For all of my days, in all of my praise
Lord it's You that I love
It's You that I love

Lord it's in You that I hope
Lord it's in You that I believe
For all of my life, in all of my nights
Lord it's in You that I hope
It's in You that I hope

For my strength Lord it's You
For my faith Lord it's You
In Your mercy Lord it's You
In Your grace Lord it's You
My Lord it's You

Lord it's in You that I trust
Lord it's in You that I will remain
For all of my years, in all of my tears
Lord it's in You that I trust
It's in You that I trust

For my strength Lord it's You
For my faith Lord it's You
In Your mercy Lord it's You
In Your grace Lord it's You
My Lord it's You

~ Canuel ~
95

We Believe

We believe, in the Prince of peace
We believe, in His saving grace

We believe, in His precious blood
We believe, that we are washed within the flood

We believe, in the power of prayer
We believe, throughout our lives He is there

We believe, in His deep nailed scars
We believe, that the sin He saves is ours

We believe, that He hears the world's cries
We believe, in His life crucified
We believe, in the silence of the upper room
We believe, in His empty tomb

We believe, in His resurrection
We believe, in the hope of Heaven

We believe, in the Garden of Gethsemane
We believe, in prayer upon our fallen knees

We believe, in His death on Calvary
We believe, in all that we cannot see
We believe, in His love upon the cross
We believe, that His death paid our cost

We believe, that we are lost within our sin
We believe, we're to be saved, born again
We believe, in His kingdom to come
We believe, the battle is already won!

We believe, that He hears the world's cries
We believe, in His life crucified
We believe, in His love upon the cross
We believe, that His death paid the cost
We believe!

~ Canuel ~
96

All to Thank You My Friend

If there's a word my words can say
I'll try to say it
If there's a prayer my soul can pray
I'll try to pray it

If there's a song my heart can sing
I'll try to sing it
If there's a joy my faith can bring
I'll try to bring it

All to thank You my friend
With all of my love, I will send
All to thank You my friend

If there's a gift my love can give
I'll try to give it
If there's a truth my life can live
I'll try to live it

If there's a peace my pain can find
I'll try to find it
If there's a light my eyes can shine
I'll try to shine it

All to thank You my friend
With all of my love, I will send
All to thank You my friend

For all the love You have shown
For all the seeds You have sown
For all the good works You have done

For all the tears You have wiped away
For all the prayers You have prayed
For all the battles You have won

All to thank You my friend
With all of my love, I will send
All to thank You my friend
Thank You my friend!

~Canuel~
97
Dedicated to my Pastor and friend,
Joseph Didonato

I Am a Christian

I kneel here, I fall upon my knees
I pray a prayer for the world, so they too might believe
I love Your love for me, although I've sinned
I tremble at the very thought, yes I am born again!
I will raise my arms, so the world can see

That I'm a Christian, and I follow You Lord
I am a Christian, and I know all You died for
I am washed within the blood
The blood of Your very life
I am a Christian, and the love of Your cross
Is here with me tonight

I now cry tears, but only tears of joy remain
I now sing this song of faith, of the love that carries my pain
I walk alone with You, upon this our common path
I talk alone with You, and I believe like I never have
I will down, so the world can see

That I'm a Christian, and I follow You Lord
I am a Christian, and I know all You died for
I am washed within the blood
The blood of Your very life
I am a Christian, and the love of Your cross
Is here with me tonight

I will raise my arms, I will bow down

That I'm a Christian, and I follow You Lord
I am a Christian, and I know all You died for
I am washed within the blood
The blood of Your very life
I am a Christian, and the love of Your cross
Is here with me tonight

~ Canuel ~
98

My Thanksgiving

For my Savior, and for Your hope
For the peace, that's in my soul
My Lord, You alone are my thanksgiving

For my prayers, and for Your light
For the love, that's in my life
My Lord, You alone are my thanksgiving

And for the faith that's, in my heart
And for the truth, that You are
Oh my Lord, My Lord
You're my thanksgiving

For my mercy, and for Your grace
For the joy, that's in my praise
My Lord, You alone are my thanksgiving

And for the faith that's, in my heart
And for the truth, that You are
Oh my Lord, My Lord
You are my thanksgiving

~ Canuel ~
99

What I Believe

At the end of the day
When I close my eyes
When it is just You
It's just You, You and I

I will stand on my faith
I'll rest in Your grace
When at last we'll stare
We will stare eye to eye, face to face

**When not what I've done
And not my battles won
When all that will matter, is what I believe**

**When this room is dark
With just the beat of one heart
When all that will matter, is what I believe**

At the end of the day
When I close my eyes
When it is just You
It's just You, You and I

~ Canuel ~
100

About the Author

Joseph Canuel resides in Greenfield, Massachusetts and has been married to his loving wife Kim for 24 years. He is the devoted father of three beautiful daughters: Jessica (age 22), Nichole, (age 22), (Yes, twins!) and Teresa (age 20).

He has always had a story in his heart that would not be silent. Joseph's family has constantly encouraged him to write. Writing has always been a part of his very soul, but it was not until he became a Christian in 1991 that his writing gained its true direction. His writing is unique with an honest and straight-from-the-heart style, speaking passionately of the truth and the love he feels for his Lord and Savior Jesus Christ!

God has laid upon his heart the desire to touch as many souls as he possibly can. Joe's writing is his life's ministry. His passionate lyrics and poems express his beliefs and his desire to share his own life experiences and God-given talents.

Joseph cannot go anywhere without his trusty pen and a folded up piece of paper, always prepared to scribble down the constant gifts of inspiration.

His heartfelt prayer is that through his writing that God's will is done. Joseph believes that it's necessary not to just to write about faith issues, but also to live out its message.

www.ingramcontent.com/pod-product-compliance
Lightning Source LLC
LaVergne TN
LVHW092317080426
835509LV00034B/731